Faces in Art

ROSEMARY MOORE

Wayland

LOOKING AT ART

Animals in Art
Faces in Art
Food in Art
Water in Art

Looking at Art is based on the *Discovering Art* series by Christopher McHugh, published by Wayland (Publishers) Ltd in 1992.

Cover: top left: *Self Portrait* by Rembrandt van Rijn, Kenwood House, London; top right: A Maori mask showing facial tattooing, Auckland Institute and Museum, New Zealand; bottom left: Olmec stone head, Anthropology Museum, Veracruz, Mexico; bottom right: *Symphonie en Rose* by Alexej von Jawlensky, Stadelsches Kunstinstitut, Frankfurt, Germany.

Editor: Deborah Elliott
Designer: Malcolm Walker
Cover design: Simon Balley

First published in 1995 by
Wayland (Publishers) Ltd.
61 Western Road, Hove
East Sussex BN3 1JD

© 1995 Wayland (Publishers) Limited

British Library Cataloguing in Publication Data
Moore, Rosemary
  Faces in Art - (Looking at Art Series)
  I. Title II. Series
704.942

ISBN 0-7502-1440-6

Typeset by Kudos, England
Printed and bound in Italy by G.Canale & C.SpA., Turin

Contents

An ancient face

The gigantic sculpture pictured on the opposite page was carved from a rock over 2,000 years ago.

The sculpture shows the face of a god. He is wearing a helmet and has earrings in his ears. The god was worshipped by the Olmec people who lived in Mexico many centuries ago.

On page 10 you can see a picture of faces painted by the Aztecs, who also lived in Mexico, but about 1,500 years after the Olmecs.

This carved stone head is in La Venta in Mexico. ▶

Faces from long ago

The picture on this page shows three people whose faces are all turned to the left. The artist who made the picture lived nearly 3,000 years ago, in a country called Sumer (now part of Iraq).

The man on the left may be a king or nobleman, or perhaps an army officer. He is being entertained by a musican playing a harp. The girl is probably a singer or dancer.

Figures from an ancient work of art called *The Standard of Ur*. It is in the British Museum in London. ▼

◄ This statue shows the head and shoulders of an Egyptian princess, called Princess Nofret. It is in the Egyptian Museum in Cairo.

The gold mask of Tutankhamun. It was found inside a pyramid at Thebes in Egypt. Now it is in the Egyptian Museum. ▼

This statue was found in an ancient tomb. It is very lifelike, with its bright painted hair and features, and eyes made from rock crystals. In fact, the workers who found it, deep inside the tomb, were terrified and ran away, believing that the figure was real.

The gold mask on the right was made for the coffin of the Egyptian king, Tutankhamun. He must have been very rich, because his tomb was full of beautiful treasures.

A bronze head of the god Apollo. It was found in Cyprus and is now in the British Museum in London. ▶

A marble bust of the Emperor Hadrian. It is in the British Museum in London. ▼

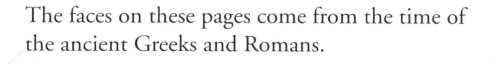

The faces on these pages come from the time of the ancient Greeks and Romans.

Above is the head of Apollo, who was the Greek god of the sun and of fertility. It was made over 2,000 years ago.

This statue was carved in marble by a Roman sculptor, about 1,500 years after the bronze head above. It is of a famous Roman emperor, Hadrian, who led his soldiers in war.

This picture of autumn decorates the floor of a large Roman house, or villa. It is called a mosaic, which is a picture made with hundreds of small, coloured stones stuck down with glue.

▲ A mosaic on the floor of a Roman villa at Cirencester in England.

Faces from around the world

The pictures on these pages were made by people living in North and South America many years ago. Below are Aztec pictures from a holy book called a *Codex*. The books are written in a kind of writing called picture writing, and show the faces of the sun god (top) and the god of darkness (below).

A page from an Aztec *Codex*. It is in the University Library in Bologna, Italy. ▼

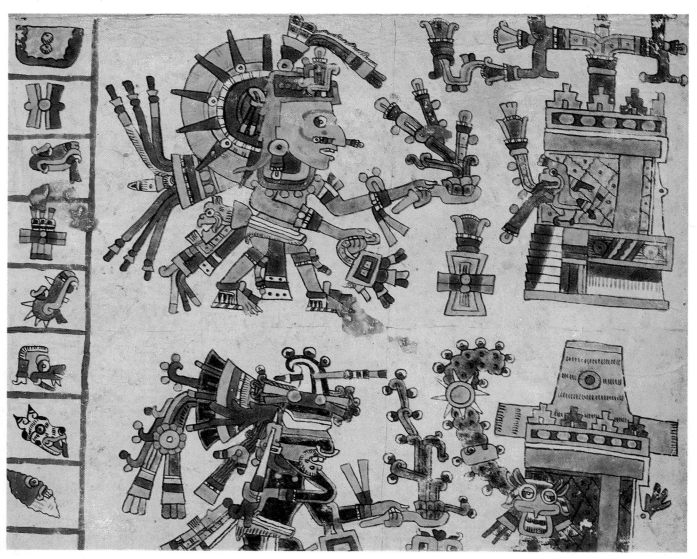

A wooden mask belonging to a girl of the Tsimshian people. It is in the Portland Art Museum in Oregon, USA.

This mask was worn by Kwakiutl Indians living in Canada. Now it is in the Field Museum of National History in Chicago, USA. ▼

Above is a wooden mask of a young North American Indian girl. The mask is very lifelike, with painted features and real hair, held in place with wooden clasps decorated as birds.

The mask on the right is also made of wood by North American Indians. Unlike the other mask, this one does not look like a real person. It seems to show a sort of 'bird man', with a strange, beak-like nose.

The faces on this page were both made in Africa. The head on the right is of a young man wearing a head-dress. He looks very lifelike. The head was made about 500 years ago.

The strange figure below was made in West Africa at about the same time as the bronze head above. It was carved in wood and covered with a sheet of metal which was decorated with patterns.

▲ A bronze head from West Africa. It is in the British Museum in London.

◄ A figure made by the BaKota people of West Africa, now in the Entwistle Gallery in London.

A Maori mask which
is in the Auckland
Institute and Museum
in New Zealand. ▶

This wooden mask comes from New Zealand.
It was carved by a Maori craftsperson. The
swirling patterns on the mask represent the
tattoos that Maori men used to have all over
their faces.

This face comes from Europe. It is about 1,000 years old and it decorates a silver cooking pot. The pot may have belonged to a Celtic prince and it was beautifully decorated, as you can see. The face is probably that of a god, and the two figures carrying animals could be hunters bringing food for the god.

The face of a Celtic god decorating the side of a silver cauldron. It is in the National Museum in Copenhagen, Denmark. ▼

◄ A bronze head of the Buddha from Thailand.

An ancient Chinese carving of the Buddha. ▼

The two faces on this page come from Asia. They are both of the Buddha, who is worshipped by many people living in India, China and other Asian countries.

Can you see that in some ways these two Buddhas are very alike? They both have calm, gentle and kind faces.

Greek and Roman faces

Thousands of years separate the three pictures on these pages. The bearded face on the right is called a mummy portrait. It was painted in Egypt 2,000 years ago, during the time of the Roman Empire. The man has a wreath on his head, which shows he was an important person.

The face below was painted 1,000 years ago. It is a picture of Jesus Christ and it is a mosaic, made with lots of tiny, coloured stones.

▲ *A Man with a Wreath*. You can see him in the National Gallery in London.

◀ A mosaic of Jesus Christ in a Church in Greece.

Jeanne Hébuterne by Amedeo Modigliani. It is in a private collection. ▶

This picture was painted quite recently, in the twentieth century. The girl is pretty, with lovely brown eyes, but the artist has made her face and neck very long. Can you see how the three faces on these pages are rather alike, with long, thin faces and rather sad eyes?

Renaissance faces

◄ The famous *Mona Lisa* by Leonardo da Vinci is in the Louvre Museum in Paris, France.

You may have seen the picture on this page before. It is one of the world's most famous paintings. It is called the *Mona Lisa*.

The *Mona Lisa* was painted by an artist called Leonardo da Vinci. He lived in Italy in the 1500s, at a time that we now call the Renaissance, or re-birth. This was a time when many wonderful paintings and sculptures were made. Leonardo's mysteriously smiling portrait has fascinated people for over 500 years.

The picture below was painted at the same time as the *Mona Lisa*, by another very famous Italian artist, called Michelangelo. It shows God leaning out from heaven, and is part of an enormous painting which Michelangelo made on the ceiling of a chapel in Rome.

Michelangelo worked for many years, lying on his back on scaffolding, high up in the roof, covering the chapel ceiling with his paintings. They tell a story from the Bible about the creation of the world.

Part of the decoration on the ceiling of the Sistine Chapel in Rome, Italy. ▶

The artist who painted this portrait was called Rogier van der Weyden. He lived a little before the time of Leonardo and Michelangelo, in the country we now call Belgium. He was one of the first artists to paint a picture of an ordinary woman.

Before the time of van der Weyden, artists in Europe nearly always painted subjects from the Bible or from ancient legends.

◄ *Portrait of a Woman* by Rogier van der Weyden. It is in the State Art Gallery in Berlin, Germany.

A self-portrait painted by Rembrandt in 1668, when he was over sixty years old. It is in Kenwood House in London. ▶

This picture was painted 200 years later than the woman opposite. It is called a self-portrait, which means the artist painted himself, looking in a mirror.

If you look closely, you will see he is holding a paint brush and a palette, on which he mixed his paints. The artist was called Rembrandt. He lived in Holland and he painted many self-portraits all through his life.

Frightening faces

This picture shows the faces of people who each feel differently about things. Four people surround Jesus Christ before he is put to death. You can see him in the middle, looking very sad. The man on the left, holding the crown of thorns, looks grim, while the man on the right seems more sympathetic. What do you think the two men at the bottom are thinking? Perhaps they are pleased about Jesus' plight.

▲ *Christ Crowned with Thorns*, by Hieronymus Bosch. It is in the National Gallery in London.

If you look closely you will see that this strange face is made up of different fruits, nuts and vegetables. How many of these can you count?

Whimsical Portrait, by Giuseppe Arcimboldo. It is in a private collection. ▶

Old Women by Francisco de Goya. It is in the Museum of Fine Art in Lille, France. ▶

Do you think the women in this picture look like witches? They were painted by a Spanish artist called Francisco de Goya. During his lifetime, the Spanish people suffered from terrible wars, and many starved or were tortured. Goya painted some of the scenes he saw or dreamed about. He thought they might make people understand the dreadful effects of war.

Modern faces

◀ *Head of a Young Girl* by Mary Cassatt. It is in the Musée de Petit Palais in Paris, France.

This picture of a little girl was drawn by the American artist Mary Cassatt. She lived in France for a long time and met many famous artists, including Vincent van Gogh, who painted the picture opposite. She used coloured crayons called pastels to make this picture.

This is a self-portrait by an artist called Vincent van Gogh. Van Gogh was Dutch but he painted many of his pictures in France, especially in the south where the sun shone with a golden light. He captured this sunlight in many of his pictures.

The self-portrait shows van Gogh with a bandaged ear, after he cut himself when he was very upset following an argument with another artist.

Self-portrait by Vincent van Gogh. You can see it in the Courtauld Institute Galleries in London. ▶

◄ *Weeping Woman* by Pablo Picasso. It is in a private collection. © DACS 1995.

This picture of a woman's face was painted in the 1920s by a famous Spanish artist called Pablo Picasso. He called the picture *Weeping Woman*. You might think this is an unusual picture of a face, but you can see how Picasso has made her look very sad. Can you see her tears rolling down her cheeks and how she is biting the corner of her handkerchief in her unhappiness?

This is what is called a modern abstract painting. Abstract means a painting that explores shapes, colours and textures as things in their own right.

Can you see how the artist has painted a face? He has used wedges and curves of colour, to show the surfaces of the features; an eye and eyebrow, the nose, the mouth and the chin.

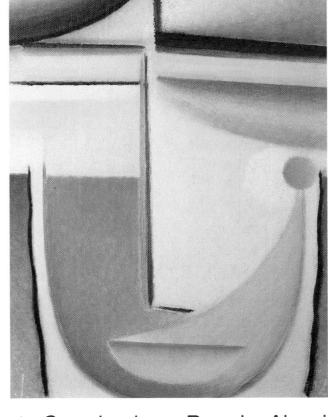

▲ *Symphonie en Rose* by Alexej von Jawlensky, in Frankfurt, Germany.

This picture shows the face of a famous American film star called Marilyn Monroe. It is a screen print, each colour made by printing separately. The black layer of the print was made from a photograph of the film star. The coloured areas show her bright lipstick and eye shadow and her blonde hair.

Marilyn by Andy Warhol.
© ARS 1995 ▶

Who are the artists?

Giuseppe Arcimboldo (1530-93) This artist lived in Milan, in Italy. He became very famous even during his lifetime, for painting faces made up of fruit, flowers and vegetables. He painted *Whimsical Portrait* on page 22.

Hieronymus Bosch (c.1450-1516) Bosch lived and worked in the Netherlands, in a town called Hertogenbosch, from which he got his name. You can see his picture *Christ Crowned with Thorns* on page 22.

Mary Cassatt (1845-1926) She was born in the USA and lived in Paris for many years. She knew some of the famous Impressionist artists who lived and worked in the city at that time. She particularly liked painting family scenes with women and children. Her drawing *Head of a Young Girl* is on page 24.

Vincent van Gogh (1853-90) Van Gogh was born in the Netherlands but painted many of his most famous pictures in France. He studied the work of earlier Dutch artists and enjoyed the work of the French Impressionists, many of whom were his friends. His paintings are famous for their brilliant colours and energetic brushwork. His self-portrait is on page 25.

Francisco de Goya (1746-1828) Goya was a Spanish artist, and he painted many pictures of the King and Queen of Spain and their family, and other important people. But he didn't always make these sorts of picture. In 1808 French armies invaded Spain, and Goya worked on a series of pictures called *The Disasters of War*, which show the cruelty and horror of war. You can see his *Old Women* on page 23.

Alexej von Jawlensky (1864-1941) Jawlensky was Russian, but he studied and worked in Germany. He formed a group of artists called the Blue Four, with three other well-known painters. His *Symphonie en Rose* is on page 27.

Leonardo da Vinci (1452-1519) Leonardo was a brilliant artist, scientist and inventor who lived in Italy during the Renaissance. He is one of the most famous artists the world has ever known. As well as making paintings and drawings, he made many scientific experiments and inventions. He was so busy all his life that very few of his paintings were completed. Even so, the works he left behind are among the greatest of the Renaissance. His famous portrait *Mona Lisa* is on page 18.

Michelangelo (Buonarroti) (1475-1564) Michelangelo is considered to be one of the greatest artists of the Renaissance, along with Leonardo and another Italian artist called Raphael. Like Leonardo, he also had many talents, and is probably best-known as a sculptor, although he was also an architect and a poet. A small detail (part) of his huge painting *The Creation* is on page 19.

Amedeo Modigliani (1884-1920) Modigliani was Italian too, but he lived many centuries later than Leonardo and Michelangelo. You can see his portrait *Jeanne Hébuterne* on page 17.

Pablo Picasso (1881-1973) Picasso was born in Spain, but after visiting Paris as a young man he decided to live in France. He was one of the most important artists of the twentieth century. With another artist called Georges Braque, he developed the style of art called Cubism. Picasso painted, drew, sculpted and even made pottery, producing an enormous number of works of art. His *Weeping Woman* is on page 26.

Rembrandt van Rijn (1606-69) Rembrandt was one of the greatest of all Dutch painters. He began his career painting pictures of stories, from ancient Greece and Rome and from the Bible. Later he made his money by painting portraits of people in Amsterdam, where he lived. Throughout his life he painted self-portraits, showing himself as he grew older. You can see the portrait he painted of himself when he was very old on page 21.

Andy Warhol (c.1928-87) Warhol was an American artist who was associated with 'Pop Art'. This type of art developed in the 1950s and 1960s, and made use of comics, advertisements and films. You can see his picture *Marilyn* on page 27.

Rogier van der Weyden (c.1399-1464) Van der Weyden was a successful artist in the fifteenth century in the town of Brussels in what is now Belgium. His paintings of people show their feelings much more than the paintings of most other painters working around him at that time. His *Portrait of a Woman* is on page 20.

Glossary

bust   A sculpture of a person's head, shoulders and chest.

Celtic   Describing the people who settled all over western Europe before the time of the Romans.

fertility   Able to produce plenty of seeds and plants.

harp   A triangular stringed musical instrument, played by plucking the strings.

Impressionists   A group of artists who were painting in France at the end of the 1800s. They were especially interested in painting the effects of light and colour in their work.

Maori   People who have lived in New Zealand since before the arrival of European settlers.

marble   A kind of white or coloured rock that can be highly polished and used for sculptures and decorations on buildings.

mosaic   A picture or pattern made by gluing pieces of coloured stone or glass on to a floor or wall.

palette   A flat piece of wood or plastic on which artists mix their colours.

Renaissance   A time in Italy, from about the 1500s to the early 1600s, when the ideas of ancient Greece and Rome were used by artists and writers.

screen print   A print made on cloth, where the ink is pressed through the weave.

tattoos   Pictures made on skin, using colours and a special needle.

textures   The feeling of the surface of objects and how this is shown in art.

Books to read

Every Picture Tells a Story by Rolf Harris (Phaidon, 1989).

Families – through the eyes of artists by Wendy and Jack Richardson (Macmillan, 1990).

History Through Art series (Wayland, 1995).

Just Look... A Book about Paintings by Robert Cumming (Viking Kestrel, 1986).

About the pictures in this book

Of course, all the pictures in this book are photographs. Some, like the Olmec head on page 5, and all the sculptures and masks, show the works exactly as the artists made them. But remember that looking at a photograph of a painting is not the same as seeing the painting itself. If possible, you should try to visit a picture gallery or museum, where you will see lots of faces made by painters, sculptors and craftspeople. You will see faces carved from wood or stone, or painted or drawn. Why not make a face yourself? Draw, paint or model your friend's face, for example.

Picture acknowledgements
The publishers have attempted to contact all copyright holders of the illustrations in this title, and apologise if there have been oversights.
The photographs in this book were supplied by: The Ancient Art and Architecture Collection © Ronald Sheridan 7 (*lower*); Bridgeman Art Library *cover* (top left, bottom right), 17, 18, 19, 20, 22 (both), 24, 27 (both). Courtauld Institute/Bridgeman 25; Giraudon/Bridgeman 23; Kenwood House/Bridgeman 21; Michael Holford © 6, 8 (top), 9, 12 (top), 16 (lower), 26. National Gallery/C.McHugh 16 (top); Werner Forman Archive *cover* (top right, bottom left), 5, 7 (top), 8 (lower), 10, 11 (both) 12 (lower), 13, 14, 15 (both). Photographs of the following paintings appear by kind permission of the copyright holders: *Weeping Woman* by Pablo Picasso, © DACS 1995; *Marilyn* by Andy Warhol. © 1995 The Andy Warhol Foundation for the Visual Arts/ARS, New York.

Index